SUMMARY

Review & Analysis of
Lakein's Book

How to Get Control of Your Time and Your Life

BusinessNews Publishing

Get instant access to more than

1,000 book summaries

Full collection at
www.mustreadsummaries.com

BOOK PRESENTATION:
GET CONTROL OF YOUR TIME AND YOUR LIFE BY ALAN LAKEIN

SUMMARY OF *GET CONTROL OF YOUR TIME AND YOUR LIFE* (ALAN LAKEIN)

BOOK PRESENTATION:
GET CONTROL OF YOUR TIME AND YOUR LIFE BY ALAN LAKEIN

BOOK ABSTRACT

MAIN IDEA

Time is life.

It's irreversible and irreplaceable. To waste your time is to waste your life, but to master your time is to master your life and to move in the direction of whatever you desire the most.

Start with a written lifetime goals statement and schedule activities that move you towards your goals, a little bit each day. Then, increasingly organize your life around your goals. Very soon, you'll be moving towards achieving your goals faster than ever you thought possible.

The biggest payoff of all in achieving control of your life and your time is greater freedom to do whatever you enjoy the most.

IMPORTANT NOTE ABOUT THIS EBOOK

This is a summary and not a critique or a review of the book. It does not offer judgment or opinion on the content of the book. This summary may not be organized chapter-wise but is an overview of the main ideas, viewpoints and arguments from the book as a whole. This means that the organization of this summary is not a representation of the book.

SUMMARY OF *GET CONTROL OF YOUR TIME AND YOUR LIFE* (ALAN LAKEIN)

SECTION 1: TIME MANAGEMENT

MAIN IDEA

An effective time management system incorporates two key elements:

1. A viable way to plan the best use of your time.
2. A way to control how your time actually gets used.

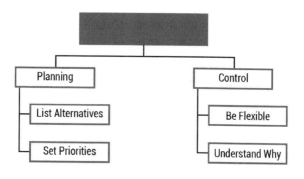

SUPPORTING IDEAS

Element #1 _ Planning

The biggest payoff in mastering your time is you gain freedom — to pursue whatever you consider to be of more importance than anything else. In the final analysis, it's your life, and you alone decide how your time should be spent. Other people may make demands, make suggestions, offer advice or even provide incentives, but those are only peripheral considerations.

There's really no such thing as a lack of time. Every person alive has the same 168 hours in a week that everyone else has. Therefore, the real question becomes how can you make certain that you are applying your available time in those areas that will deliver the greatest benefits?

Time management is quite an individual choice. Some people are comfortable letting life meander along without direction and stability. Others like to be firmly in control, making conscious decisions about everything they do. Again, there's no absolute right or wrong approach — just a matter of personal preference.

The best time control systems are well balanced. If time management is too tight, people can become compulsive and obsessive about the way they spend their time. By contrast, a time management system that is loose leads to apathy, indifference and frustration as nothing meaningful is accomplished. Balance is a critical quality for a good time management system.

There are three types of time conscious people that should be avoided as far as possible:

1. Over-organizers — People who are always fooling around with lists of things to do. They end up spending so much time considering all the angles that frequently they become paralyzed and forget to get into action. These people plan things to the finest detail. They feel a sense of accomplishment just by being organized — so much so, in fact, that what's achieved gets lost in the shuffle. Over-organizers are blind to new opportunities, ongoing changes and the changing need of people they interact with.

2. Hyperactive — People who mistake activity for achievement. In their rush to fill every minute with activity, they never take the time to evaluate the worth of whatever they are doing. In other words, they're so busy clamoring up the tree they don't even notice they should be climbing another tree altogether.

3. Time Nuts — People who are overwhelmingly preoccupied with never wasting a fraction of a minute. These people constantly set for themselves an impossible schedule. They are always in a rush trying to catch up to where they think they should be. The telltale sign of a Time Nut is they keep detailed records, going back months or years, of how every minute was spent.

Each of these groups of people have taken a potentially valuable trait and turned it into a liability simply by placing an undue emphasis on it. Effective time management is far more balanced than that. Ideally, a good time management system will aid rather than impede productivity. It will be responsive to changing needs, flexible enough to allow some breathing space and powerful enough to take into account all the dimensions of a person's life.

Planning how to use your time effectively is a two-step process:

1. Make a list of all available possibilities.
   This step is usually quite straightforward. Do this in writing if you want it to be useful. Take a blank piece of paper and list all your future alternatives. To be of any value, the list must be comprehensive and complete, with every alternative written down.

2. Set priorities — by your own personal criteria.
   Go through your list and give everything a grade:
   A — items that will provide the greatest personal satisfaction.
   B — items that are important but not vital or essential.
   C — Items that can be postponed without any bad effects.
   Now make up a second list which contains just those items you rank as A's. Rank them in order of importance: A-1, A-2, A-3 and so on through the list.
   Now rewrite your list of A priority projects:

```
┌────────────────────────────────────┐
│              My Projects             │
│ ──────────────────────────────────  │
│  A - 1                               │
│ ──────────────────────────────────  │
│  A - 2                               │
│ ──────────────────────────────────  │
│  A - 3                               │
│ ──────────────────────────────────  │
│  A - 4                               │
│ ──────────────────────────────────  │
│  A - 5                               │
└────────────────────────────────────┘
```

To be effective, this list will need to be updated regularly – monthly, weekly or even daily depending on your own preferences.

Keep in mind your priorities will vary from time to time, depending on your circumstances and external events. Priorities also vary over time – today's A-3 may be tomorrow's A-1 as a deadline approaches.

Also acknowledge nobody else can determine your priorities for you. This is an intensely personal project. You might take into account the opinions and ideas of others. Other people might factor large in some of the projects you put on your list. But the final decision and ranking as to which items are of the highest priority is yours alone.

Element #2   Control

When it comes to making decisions about how to spend your time, the decision making process always is exceptionally difficult. There are always more choices than can ever be satisfied. There are always some elements of the use of our time over which we have no control. And quite frequently there are intense competing needs which cannot be satisfied simultaneously. All of these decisions are difficult.

When you stop and think about why and how people make decisions about their use of time, there are several possibilities:

- Force of habit – they've been doing things that way for most of their life, therefore, they assume that's the way things will always be done in the future.
- Demands of other people – they do things to make someone else happy or possibly to avoid irritating them.
- Escapism – they like to daydream about what would be nice rather than getting into action.
- Spur of the moment – they decide to do something spontaneously because of an unexpected opportunity.
- Default _ they wait for others to make the first move.
- Conscious decision – they work to a plan and accomplish what they have identified as a high value objective.

At various times, there may be nothing wrong with making decisions for any of these reasons. From a long-term perspective, however, the more a person can make conscious decisions, the more they will achieve.

Controlling how you use your time is a two-step process:

1. Retain some flexibility – the more the better.
   There's only one thing you can absolutely guarantee about the way you use your time – things won't go as planned 100-percent of the time. Therefore, build some flexibility into your time management system.
   That way, when unexpected or unanticipated events crop up, they don't end up derailing your entire life.
2. Focus on the reasons why projects have the importance rating they do.
   A good way to restore enthusiasm for any project is to periodically stop and think a little about the reasons why that project is on your A- list.
   If there are genuine benefits to be derived, you'll have no trouble remembering them and dwelling on them. The more vivid you can make those benefits appear, the greater the motivation you'll generate for regaining forward momentum again.
   If you can't visualize the tangible benefits you'll derive, stop and give yourself a reality check. You might even want to revisit your planning activities and check whether or not you were accurate in the priorities you set. That lack of visualization may be a mental clue you're heading off on a tangent, or focusing on some-

thing that will deliver only marginal benefits, rather than something that is of greater significance.

Again, focusing on the reasons why you want to achieve something should provide great motivation and will-power. People who are working on something they are intensely interested in feel refreshed and invigorated the more time they spend. There will be a general air of excitement and energy in every minute they spend.

SECTION 2: GOALS

MAIN IDEA

Everyone should prepare a lifetime goals statement that is constantly being changed and updated as priorities and tastes change and as new opportunities become available.

SUPPORTING IDEAS

To prepare a lifetime goals statement, follow these steps:

Step #1 _ Prepare

Go somewhere where you can think clearly and where you won't be disturbed. Take a supply of paper, a watch and a pen.

Step #2 _ List all the possibilities

What Are My
Lifetime Goals?

Take a blank sheet of paper, head it up as shown above and spend a full three to five minutes filling the page with as many ideas as you can. Don't try and stifle your thinking at this stage. Write down every idea that comes to mind, no matter how impractical it may seem.

Then take another five minutes to look at each of the goals you've written down, and make any changes you like.

Step #3 _ Narrow your time frame

How Would I Like
To Spend
The Next 3 Years?

Again, take about three to five minutes to list everything that comes to mind in response to that question. As for the first exercise, suspend judgement at this stage, and list everything you can think of.

As before, take a similar amount of time (three to five minutes) to review what you've written and make changes where required, or add in what was left out.

Step #4 _ The immediate future

```
┌─────────────────────────────┐
│                             │
│      If I Knew I Would Be    │
│      Struck By Lightning     │
│         In 6 Months Time,    │
│        How Would I Live      │
│           Until Then?        │
│                             │
│                             │
│                             │
│                             │
│                             │
│                             │
│                             │
│                             │
└─────────────────────────────┘
```

In filling in this sheet, assume all your funeral arrangements are taken care of. List how you would live and what you would do if you were faced with news of your imminent demise.

As usual, take between three and five minutes to fill the sheet in, and a similar amount of time to review what you've written.

Step #5 _ Now have another go at your lifetime goals

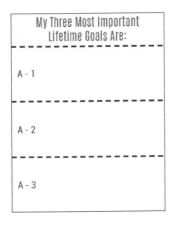

My Three Most Important
Lifetime Goals Are:

A - 1

A - 2

A - 3

Taking the other sheets you've already filled out, try and clarify your three most important lifetime goals.

How should conflicts be resolved? Keep in mind these ideas:

- Conflicts are good. They encourage you to work hard on increasing the value of your time, which in turn maximizes the achievements of your life. You'll suddenly realize there are lots of good things you can and should accomplish — therefore, you don't have a minute to spare.
- Conflicts are resolved by priorities. You have to decide that achieving one goal is worth the time that could be

spent in every other area.
- Keep in mind your priorities will change over time. Therefore, goals are written on paper – not carved on marble tablets.
- If you can't assign a higher priority to one goal over another, then you know you should be allocating equal amounts of time to each goal.

Keep refining your thoughts until you come up with the three goals that mean the most to you, in order of importance. This will probably take six or seven attempts to get right. Don't get frustrated – getting this right is well worth the time and effort, because it will color everything else you do.

Step #6 _ List specific activities for each lifetime goal

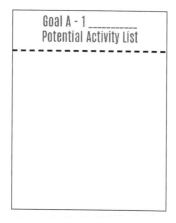

You can't do a goal. You can only do activities that ultimately will lead to achieving the overall goal. Thus, you need to make a separate list of every potential activity that will lead towards each lifetime goal.

Again, list everything and leave censorship or selection until the next step. Take about three to five minutes for each lifetime goal, using a separate sheet of paper for each. Then take a similar amount of time to review what you've written.

Be creative and imaginative in this step.'

Step #7 _ Select high priority activities

In this step, you switch your emphasis from being creative to being practical. Specifically, you need to write down the answers to one key question. For each activity listed in step #6, ask yourself:

- "Am I committed to spending a minimum of five minutes on this activity in the next seven days?"

If you are not, cross that activity off your list. (Note: You don't have to give any reason for crossing something off the list – the choice is yours alone using whatever criteria you choose).

For those activities that are left, you then set priorities – decide which activity is the most important through to which has the least importance. For each goal, you then make up a list of activities, and schedule a time within the next seven days to work on that activity:

Goal A - 1 _____ Activity Schedule	
Activity	Time
A - 1	
A - 2	
A - 3	
A - 4	
A - 5	

Make up a separate sheet for your A-1, A-2 and A-3 lifetime goals. These sheets can be reviewed and changed each week. You may want to keep these sheets somewhere close and then cross off activities as they are completed or do something similar to highlight progress.

Step #8 _ The Weekly Planning Session

Now that you've completed clarifying your goals, weekly planning becomes simple and straight forward. Take a few minutes every week to:

1. Review your lifetime goals statement

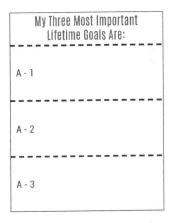

2. Schedule activities for your goals in the next week

Goal A - 1 _____ Activity Schedule	
Activity	Time
A - 1	
A - 2	
A - 3	
A - 4	
A - 5	

Goal A - 2 _____ Activity Schedule	
Activity	Time
A - 1	
A - 2	
A - 3	
A - 4	
A - 5	

Goal A - 3 _____ Activity Schedule	
Activity	Time
A - 1	
A - 2	
A - 3	
A - 4	
A - 5	

If you keep these activity planning sheets somewhere where you will see them every day and where you can cross off activities as they are completed, you'll maximize the results you achieve. Your focus every week then becomes to find creative ways to maximize the amount of time spent on activities that are directly related to your lifetime goals.

Do that consistently week in and week out and you'll be surprised and pleased by the amount of progress you can actually make.

SECTION 3: SCHEDULING YOUR TIME

MAIN IDEA

Scheduling is the link between what you'd like to do and what you ultimately end up doing.

To improve your scheduling performance:

1. Understand where demands on your time originate.
2. Invest time in planning.
3. Find ways to work smarter, not harder.
4. Make use of "TO DO" lists.
5. Apply the 80-20 Rule.

SUPPORTING IDEAS

1. Understand where demands on your time originate.

Demands on time typically come from two different directions:

1. Those we have no control over – daily routines, prior commitments or the everyday, essential tasks of your personal or professional life.
2. Discretionary decisions – where you set a goal and then allocate available time to work towards that goal.

Scheduling is the vital link that helps hit the best possible balance between these demands. The less time you have available, the more you need to plan effectively. You'll always come out ahead in the long run if you invest a little time in scheduling.

The two key times for scheduling are:

- Mornings – when you're fresh.
- Evenings – when the days is still fresh in your mind.

Both times have advantages and disadvantages, so usually the best approach is to make use of both.

2. Invest time in planning.

In laying out your schedule, the objective is to set aside time for working on your A-priority activities. You can do this by:

- Reserving a particular day for A-priority activities alone.
- Having a specific time each day where you work only on A-activities.
- Designating a weekly time slot for A- activities.
- Getting your daily, routine tasks completed on a same time, each day basis. This reduces indecision and generates additional energy and enthusiasm. It also establishes good work habits. There is always enough time to do whatever you consider is most important. Scheduling allows you to create the time to do what's

important at the expense of what's not.
- Everyone has two kind of prime time – internal and external. Internal prime time is when you work best. External prime time is the best time to work in with other people. Schedule whichever of your activities require creativity to internal prime time, and whichever activities require cooperation with others to external prime time. Never put routine tasks in either internal or external prime time.
- Don't try and fill every minute of your schedule. That will just generate frustration. Leave large gaps for the unexpected things that continually crop up – at least an hour a day.
- If at all possible, try and get anything that is a "Must Do" out of the way as quickly as possible each day.

Ideally, a good time schedule will be a dynamic balance of scheduled and unscheduled time. That way, your life will flow smoothly.

3. Find ways to work smarter, not harder.

You'll be surprised at how much time you can actually find to work towards your goals if you plan smarter rather than try and work harder. Try these ideas:

- Cater to your individuality rather than against it.
  Some people actually achieve more by having large blocks of free time, after which they get back to work refreshed and full of energy. Others like to have tight

schedules, where every minute is filled with activity. Neither way is "right" or "wrong". Just find out what works for you, and then maximize the amount of time those conditions are created. If you're not certain which approach fits your personality, experiment a little and keep track of how it works out.

- Look at your transition time.
  This is the time you spend between when you get up and when you arrive at work, and then again from the time you leave work until you go to sleep. Are there some things that you can be doing to improve the quality of this time? Some ideas which others have used:

  ° Use this time for planning the day ahead.
  ° Find ways to be learning something new each day.
  ° Try listening to tapes while doing something else.
  ° Set up some good hobbies, and get actively involved.

- Look at your commuting time.
  What can you do to make this time productive? Is it feasible to move closer to your work? Can you listen to tapes that educate and inform rather than spend time being entertained? Talk to other people, and find out what they've done in this area.

- Think about your coffee breaks.
  This may be an ideal time to get one or two rapid fire activities closely aligned with your personal goals out of the way each day. The change of pace will be just as refreshing as taking a complete break. You'll be amazed at how much you can do in just a few minutes

every day.

- How about your lunch breaks?
  This is a good time to set aside for an activity that's fun, entertaining and productive, without being disturbed.
- Have you ever tried to make your sleep work for you?
  Try posing a question to your subconscious mind when you go to sleep. Write it down. Then, when you wake up, review the question you wrote down. It will amaze you what your subconscious can contribute, given half a chance.
- Think about Parkinson's Law.
  This law states: *"Work expands to fill the time allowed for its completion"*. To repeal Parkinson's Law, you have to look for ways to increase efficiency, and keep on setting shorter and shorter deadlines for yourself. You should also become keenly aware of the time spent on routine tasks. Look for ways to progressively decrease that time period, otherwise it will creep up and up.
- Keep a spare "special emphasis" task close at hand.
  Everyone gets a little unanticipated spare time each day. Quite often, people aren't organized enough to take advantage of those spare moments. Think ahead. Have something close at hand that is aligned with your goals, and that you can pick up and then drop at a moment's notice. Whenever, you get some unanticipated free time, use it on something productive.

4. Make use of "TO DO" lists.

A "TO DO" list _ with items in order of priority _ is a key tool in making the best available use of your time.

To put together a worthwhile "TO DO" list:

- Write everything down. Then you can relax and concentrate on getting things done instead of trying to remember what needs to be done.
- Cross off items that are completed. That gives you a great feeling of moving ahead.
- Add new items as they occur to you at the bottom of the list.
- Once a day, prioritize your list. Rewrite it, with the highest priority items at the top. Then work from the top. That way, you'll be making the best possible use of your time.
- Discipline yourself to work through your list.

5. Apply the 80-20 Rule.

The 80-20 Rule states:

> "If all items are arranged in order of value, 80% of the value will come from 20% of the items."

From a time management perspective, the 80-20 Rule can be used to increase productivity. In essence, you should identify those items which provide the bulk of the added value created, and do those things. At that point, you then evaluate whether or not it will be worth completing the rest of the items. Quite often, you'll find there will be no compelling reason to complete the rest of the items.

To put this another way, consider a list which has A-priority, B-priority and C-priority items:

- One of the best ways to find more time for A's is to avoid C's. Therefore, look through your list for an C's that can be crossed off without any problems. Cross off those C's.
- Look carefully at each C that remains. Can it be upgraded to an A or a B somehow? If not, it can probably be crossed off without any problems. Go ahead and do that and again you've freed up more time.
- Keep the materials you need for your A's and B's somewhere close at hand. Keep the materials for your C's stored somewhere else. That way, whenever you have a few spare minutes, it will be easier to get moving on your A's or B's than it will on the C's.

The 80-20 Rule also applies to the way you sort your incoming mail. Many people make the mistake of lingering over this daily task for marginal if any productive results. To optimize your handling of incoming mail:

- Keep three folders into which mail is sorted:
  ◦ Action – for items that must be attended to.
  ◦ Information – for things you should read.

° Deferred — for things you want to think about.

- Classify everything as it comes in into one of those three folders, or throw it away.
- Try and handle each piece of paper once only and move on to the next item.
- Write informal notes in reply and photocopy that before sending it if necessary.
- Periodically go through your "Information" and "Deferred" folders and throw away material that is not needed.

SECTION 4: 13 SPECIFIC TIME TECHNIQUES

MAIN IDEA

To enhance your productivity, try these ideas and strategies:

1. Learn how to accommodate other people's needs.
2. Create quiet time for yourself.
3. Ask Lakein's Question.
4. Use the Swiss cheese method.
5. Find some instant tasks.
6. Try changing your motivation.
7. Slow down rather than speed up.
8. Get around your fears.
9. Set yourself a deadline.
10. Stress the benefits, not the pain.
11. Get back on track if you procrastinate.
12. Just a few minutes more.

13. Do your best and be happy with that.

SUPPORTING IDEAS

1. Learn how to accommodate other people's needs.

While we all like to help others, you shouldn't do so at the expense of something that's important. There isn't enough time to have every piece of candy in the store. Therefore, set your priorities and stick to them, even when others try to soak up your available time.

Never say "yes" if you mean "no". Saying "no" promptly but politely saves time in the long run. You might even consider taking the person aside and explaining your priorities and the reasons for saying no.

Always stay on the lookout for quick compromises that will get tasks done promptly.

2. Create quiet time for yourself.

If you consistently find interruptions coming along to stop you getting some quality time for yourself to think creatively, try these ideas:

- If the interruptions come from your boss, let him / her know about the problem. Discuss the possibility of delegating to someone else. Align your priorities and your boss's priorities and the interruptions should end.

- If it's subordinates who are interrupting, schedule a regular consultation session. Have a scheduled time where subordinates can meet with you, and then stick to it. They'll get the idea fairly quickly.

3. Ask Lakein's Question.

Lakein's question is: *"What is the best use of my time right now?"*

Invariably, whatever is your first, spontaneous answer will be the correct one. Use this question to find your highest priority and motivate yourself to stick to your high priority tasks.

You should be result oriented rather than time oriented. Stay on the lookout for more effective ways to get everything done. Always keep at the forefront of your thinking the 80/20 Rule – that 80-percent of the value in most projects comes from 20-percent of the task. That means that 80-percent of another task may be worth much more than the remaining 20-percent of the current task.

If you ask Lakein's question often, you can avoid drifting aimlessly along life's highways.

4. Use the Swiss cheese method.

Sometimes, an A-1 task can seem overwhelming. To off-set that perception, use the Swiss Cheese Method:

- Try and identify why you are procrastinating. Some-times, just identifying the cause of your reluctance and addressing that will do the trick and get you moving again.
- Find an instant task somewhere in your A-1 – some-thing that will only take five minutes or so. Then do one of these instant tasks each day. You'll be surprised at how often once you start doing something even just for 5 minutes, the momentum will start building and you'll soon be working on your A-1 for extended periods of time.

5. Find some instant tasks.

To get into action on your A-1 projects, try these ideas:

- Do some detailed planning.
  Take out a blank piece of paper, head it up, "I Have Decided..." and the map out your plan of attack. Then leave the paper somewhere where you'll see it every day.
- Get more information.
  If you just can't seem to get started, try getting more information together. Often, putting the background material together will make it easier to get rolling.
- Find a leading task.
  A good leading task will generate an incredible feeling

of achievement and involvement. Find a good leading task and set out a time you'll complete it. Then do it.

- Use your current mood.
From time to time, your mood might be upbeat and full of energy. Whenever that happens, seize the moment and plunge enthusiastically into your A-1. You may be surprised by how much you can actually achieve while the mood suits you.
- Give yourself a pep talk.
Many high performers give themselves a bit of verbal self-encouragement. Try it. Remind yourself that you won't know for a fact how hard something is until you do it, so give it a go and see how it all pans out.
- Make a commitment to someone else.
If you make a promise to a friend, that can serve as a motivator – especially if they keep on asking you about it.

6. Try changing your motivation.

To keep going on your A-1, even if you feel like quitting:

- Never stop working on your A-1 until you have mapped

out the next step. That keeps up your momentum.
- Add some variety. Try doing something different which is still heading in the right direction.
- Look hard for something new and exciting about your A-1.
- Take a short break and come back at it again refreshed.
- Change your information level. Add more information to get moving again. Or lose a little bit of information so the big picture becomes clear again.

7. Slow down rather than speed up.

At the key pivotal points on a project, stop and take mental stock of your options. If you make a conscious decision to move forward at that point after thinking everything through clearly and dispassionately, you can then move forward with enthusiasm and commitment.

Enjoy the decision you've made. Don't revisit it again and again. Concentrate on doing.

8. Get around your fears.

Fear can stand directly in the path of success. If you notice fear is present, stop and ask yourself: *"What is it I'm afraid of here?"*

Often, just the simple step of doing that will be all that's needed. If that doesn't work, however, you can try and counterbalance your fears by:

- Giving yourself a mental pep talk.
- Concentrating on the present, not on some potential scenario that might or might not play out in the future.
- Trying mental judo. The idea of judo is to use your opponent's strength against him. Look for potential problems, and find ways to turn them into strong points. That way, anything you fear becomes your strong point.
- Balloon your fears out of all proportion. Let your imagination run riot. Pretty soon, you'll realize the world will not stop revolving, even if the thing you fear most plays out the worst possible way. Therefore, relax.

9. Set yourself a deadline.

Sometimes, just the pressure of a looming deadline will provide loads of motivation – even if the deadline is a self-imposed one. In fact, whenever you beat a deadline, you feel great. It builds up your self-confidence and delivers a feeling of achievement.

Therefore, set deadlines in everything you do. You'll feel better, get more done and avoid the hassles only procrastination can generate.

10. Stress the benefits, not the pain.

A positive approach _ stressing the benefits of action _ is always more motivating than dwelling on the negatives that will result from inactivity. Ideally, you want to be so busy thinking about the benefits that you won't even have time to ponder anything negative.

A great way to stress the benefits is to reward yourself when you've achieved something meaningful. The better the reward, the more you'll feel motivated. Set high goals, decide on some great rewards and then work hard to be able to realize those rewards.

If at all possible, try and turn whatever you need to do into a game. Have fun while you see how quickly you can get the task completed. Set up a scorecard somewhere where you'll see it every day. Try and put together a long winning streak while you build up some solid achievements day-in and day-out. Before too long, your life will be full of rewarding activities that are aligned with your lifetime goals.

11. Get back on track if you procrastinate.

If you've succumbed to the temptation to procrastinate or waste a little time, try these ideas on getting back to your A-1 task again:

- Have a pep talk with yourself – like a coach's talk at halftime. Tell yourself it's decision time.
- Program yourself so that when you are avoiding your A-1, you say to yourself: "I'm wasting my time here."

Sooner or later, you'll get sick of wasting your time and get back to work.

- Cut off all your escape routes. Do everything you can to eliminate those tempting little tasks that can soak up time and drain your productivity.
- Procrastinate whole heartedly. In other words, if you're determined to waste time, sit in a chair and do nothing for 20-minutes. Before too long, you'll feel an over-whelming desire to get back into action.

12. Just a few minutes more.

Whenever you're working on an A-1 priority task and it comes time to quit, discipline yourself to work just 5-minutes more on that project. That way, you'll gradually, over time, build your expertise and know-how. If you keep to this rule, before long you'll become very good at sticking to whatever needs to be done.

13. Do your best and be happy with that.

Studies have shown that people who hoped and strived for success are happier and accomplish more than those who fear failure. If you're willing to accept some initial failures on your way to success, you'll often find the energy to keep going until you strike pay dirt.

Instead of focusing on minimizing losses, try to maximize successes. Remember, when you try something you've never attempted before, you're laying the groundwork to do better the next time around. However it pans out, you'll be further ahead than if you'd done nothing.

Life can only be lived on a best efforts basis. Don't worry about the past. Work hard in the present. Remember, whatever the past, your future is still spotless.

What is the best use of my time right now?

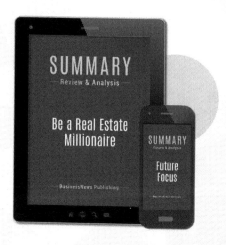

Made in the USA
Middletown, DE
16 May 2020

94774024R00024